AN INDIAN BOOK

Tecumseh: Shawnee Warrior-Statesman

BY JAMES McCAGUE
ILLUSTRATED BY VICTOR DOWD

ABOUT THE BOOK: The story of Tecumseh, the great Shawnee leader who dreamed and worked for a strong, united Indian nation, is told here with warmth and feeling. Tecumseh's early life and efforts to organize his people in the face of the white man's encroachment, receives the emphasis in this biography that provides a lesson in brotherhood and understanding. This is one of Garrard's INDIAN BOOKS, which give young readers, through biographies of individual Indians, a clearer understanding of the role the Indians played in the growth of America.

Subject classification: Social Studies, American History, Biography
Sub-classification: Reading, Information, War of 1812

ABOUT THE AUTHOR: James McCague is well-known in the book field as an adult novelist and historian. In most of his books for adults and children, he integrates in lively style the elements of history and transportation. Born in Chicago, raised in a family of railroad men, and educated at Northwestern University, McCague has written six other books for Garrard, all in the HOW THEY LIVED series. *Tecumseh* is his first book in the INDIAN series.

Reading Level: Grade 3
80 pages . . . 6½ x 8¾

Interest Level: Grades 2–5
Publisher's Price: 3.40

SBN 8116-6607-7

Illustrated in color; full-color jacket; reinforced binding

GARRARD PUBLISHING COMPANY

TECUMSEH
SHAWNEE WARRIOR-STATESMAN

BY JAMES McCAGUE

ILLUSTRATED BY VICTOR DOWD

GARRARD PUBLISHING COMPANY
CHAMPAIGN, ILLINOIS

ALICE MARRIOTT and CAROL K. RACHLIN of Southwest Research Associates are consultants for Garrard Indian Books. They are presently joint artists-in-residence in the Division of Language Arts at Central State College, Edmond, Oklahoma.

MISS MARRIOTT has lived among the Kiowa and Cheyenne Indians in Oklahoma and spent many years with the Pueblos of New Mexico and the Hopis of Arizona. First woman to take a degree in anthropology from the University of Oklahoma, she is a Fellow of the American Anthropological Association, now working with its Curriculum Project.

MISS RACHLIN, also a Fellow of AAA and of the American Association for the Advancement of Science, is a graduate in anthropology of Columbia University. She has done archaeological work in New Jersey and Indiana, and ethnological field work with Algonquian tribes of the Midwest.

Contents

The Shawnees

Tecumseh's people, the Shawnee Indians, were an Algonquian tribe who had, at an earlier time, migrated from the East to Ohio River country. The tribe was divided into clans, each of which had its own chief and governed itself. On important matters the clans acted together.

Each Shawnee clan lived in a large village of roomy wigwams. Each wigwam had a framework made of bent poles, which was covered by cat-tail mats in summer and slabs of birch bark in winter. They could be easily taken down and moved, when necessary.

An agricultural people, the Shawnees grew corn, hunted game, and once a year traveled to the western plains to hunt buffalo. They wore skin clothing, used woven baskets, pottery containers, and wooden bowls and spoons.

In earlier years they had traveled by foot or in dugout canoes. In Tecumseh's time, they rode horses as well.

1. Kispoko Town, where Tecumseh lived as a boy

2. The Ohio River, where young Tecumseh attacked
   a flatboat carrying settlers into Shawnee country

3. Vincennes, where Governor Harrison met with Tecumseh
   and tried to stop the Indians from banding together

4. Prophet's Town, where Tenskatawah disobeyed
   Tecumseh and attacked Harrison's men

5. Detroit, which Tecumseh and his Indian warriors
   helped the British capture in the War of 1812

6. The battlefield where Tecumseh was killed

1

A Day of Sorrow

Six-year-old Tecumseh sat up in bed and rubbed his eyes. It was a chilly October morning in 1774.

Tecumseh had been dreaming that the Long Knives were chasing him. They were strange, pale-faced men with swords like large hunting knives, who came from a land far to the east. He was glad it was only a dream.

Then all of a sudden he shivered. The dream could come true!

Years before, the Long Knives had made a treaty with Tecumseh's people, the Shawnees. They had promised to stay away from the Indian lands north of the great Ohio River. Recently, however, they had broken their promise and started to settle in Shawnee country.

Just a few days ago, the Shawnees had heard that an army of Long Knives was on the march to attack them. Tecumseh's father, chief of one of the five Shawnee clans, and his big brother, Chiksika, had gone off to fight that army. All the warriors in their village had gone too. Since then, there had been no news.

All at once Tecumseh heard dogs barking and people running all about outside his bark-covered wigwam. Beside him his little brother <u>Lowalusika</u> woke up. Lowalusika was only three years old. He was frightened and began to cry.

Throwing back the buffalo robe that covered their bed, Tecumseh ran outside. The boys lived in a village on the banks of the Scioto River, in the land now called Ohio. In those long-ago times, all of Ohio belonged to the Shawnees and other Indian tribes.

A big crowd had gathered in the center of the village around a group of warriors. As Tecumseh ran to join them, an old man hobbled past. "Hou!" he shouted. "It's all over."

Tecumseh's heart sank. He saw his older sister, Tecumapase, trying to give comfort to their mother, Methotasa. The tears streamed down Methotasa's face.

Tecumseh's beloved seventeen-year-old brother, Chiksika, was there too.

Chiksika was tall and strong and already a warrior. Under the stripes of red, yellow, and blue warpaint, his face was sad. He came and put his hand on Tecumseh's shoulder.

"Bad news, little brother. Our father, Chief Pucksinwah, is dead."

Tecumseh felt numb inside. He couldn't answer.

"There was a great battle by the Ohio River," said Chiksika. "We fought bravely and killed many Long Knives, but a bullet pierced Pucksinwah's heart. We fought on for a while without him, but then more of the Long Knives came. There were too many of them. We had to run away."

Tecumseh shut his eyes tightly. He was a chief's son; no one must see him cry. "What will happen now?" he asked.

Chiksika shook his head. "The great chief of all the Shawnees has called a council to decide whether we should fight on. Many of our people think that the Long Knives are too strong. They say we must give up now."

"Never!" shouted Tecumseh. He lifted his chin high. "I will go and fight the Long Knives myself and kill them all!"

His big brother smiled gently. "Those are big words for a small warrior only six summers old," he said. "Be patient, boy. Your time will come."

2

Growing-up Years

"Our people have made peace with the Long Knives," Chiksika said to Tecumseh one day later that autumn. It was a good peace. The white men agreed to keep their old promise and stay south of the Ohio River. Thus, all the land north of the river was left to the Indians.

"We can be friends now," said many Shawnees.

As time went by, however, the white men broke their word once more. Long Knives crossed the Ohio River and built cabins. They shot Indians who went near them. In return, fierce Shawnee warriors started to raid the white settlements.

Tecumseh still longed to be able to join the warriors. For the moment, though, he was busy learning to fish, to trap small animals, and to paddle a canoe. He wrestled and played games with other boys his age.

When Tecumseh was twelve years old he made a new friend, Sinninatha. He was a white boy who had been captured and adopted into the Shawnee tribe. Sinninatha seemed content to be a Shawnee. He was always so cheerful and pleasant that Tecumseh couldn't help liking him.

One evening as they sat by the village campfire, Tecumseh asked, "Did you have a Long-Knife name, Sinninatha?"

The other boy nodded. "Yes. Stephen Ruddell."

"It sounds funny," Tecumseh laughed. Then he began to point at various things nearby. "*Acohqua*," he said. "*Il-le-nah-lui. Weshe.* What are those in Long-Knife talk?"

Sinninatha had to think hard, for it had been a long time since he had spoken English. At last he named each thing: "Kettle. Arrow. Dog."

A strange excitement took hold of Tecumseh. "You must teach me this talk," he cried.

"Well, all right. But why?"

"I don't know, but you must," Tecumseh said. To himself he thought, "The Long Knives are my enemies, and it is good to know all we can about our enemies."

Sinninatha jumped up and ran to his hut. He came back with a small, leather-covered object. "This is a book—an English Bible," he explained. "Some warriors took it from a cabin they burned not long ago, but they don't know what it's for. Do you?"

"Book?" Tecumseh frowned. "Bi-bel?"

Sinninatha opened the book. "See these marks. They stand for words, as if the person who made the marks is speaking to you. In this way the words are never forgotten."

Tecumseh clapped a hand over his mouth in amazement. He turned the book's pages. "Long Knives must be very wise," he said thoughtfully. "There is great power in such a thing. I will learn these marks also."

And so he did. He studied until he could speak English almost as well as Sinninatha. Reading and writing were harder, but Tecumseh practiced every day and in time he became fairly good at both.

These were busy years for Tecumseh. Chiksika was training him to use bow and arrow, tomahawk and warclub. He taught the boy to ride a horse and to hunt deer, bear, and buffalo. From his big brother, too, Tecumseh learned the meaning of honor.

"Only weak people can lie or cheat," Chiksika told his brother. "Remember that always."

Sometimes Lowalusika joined in the lessons. The youngest brother was growing into a scrawny, ugly little boy. Even worse, he was lazy. "I won't work! I'll use my wits," he boasted. "Who wants to be a warrior, anyway?"

Tecumseh was fond of his little brother, but such talk made him angry. Chiksika calmed Tecumseh. "Let him alone," he would say. "Each of you must decide for himself what kind of man he will be."

3

The Long Knives

Chiksika sent for Tecumseh one day. "You have seen fifteen summers and fifteen winters," he said. "You are old enough now to put on warpaint. Will you come with us to raid the Long Knives?"

Tecumseh's heart pounded. He had worked hard to become a warrior. "Now I will prove myself," he thought as he ran eagerly to get his weapons.

With Chiksika in the lead, the small band of Shawnees rode south to the Ohio River. White settlers coming to Indian country often floated downriver in flatboats. The war party decided to attack the first boat that came along.

They were in luck. A scout soon brought word that a flatboat had landed some distance upstream. Tecumseh crept silently along the riverbank with the other warriors. Then he saw the Long Knives through the bushes. They were cooking their supper over a campfire.

Tecumseh counted thirteen men. They all had guns. He felt chills run up and down his back. "Be strong!" he told himself fiercely. "Be brave!"

Chiksika aimed his long rifle. *Bang*! A white man sprawled on the ground.

Instantly, every warrior yelled out the shrill Shawnee war cry. Other rifles cracked. Tecumseh pulled his bowstring. His arrow flew straight and true. Down went a white man standing by the fire.

Tecumseh ran toward the enemy. A bullet whistled past his ear. A big Long Knife swung his rifle at him like a club. Another warrior struck the Long Knife. Carefully, he aimed his tomahawk. . . .

Suddenly it was all over. White men were strewn on the ground. Some Shawnees were wounded, but not one had been killed.

"You did well, brother!" Chiksika cried. "How does it feel to be a warrior?"

To tell the truth, Tecumseh felt dazed. The fight had been like a wild dream.

But his heart nearly burst with pride at Chiksika's praise.

"Hou!" called one of the warriors. "Here's one that's still alive." He stood over the white man who was trying feebly to crawl away.

Several warriors seized the wounded man. They dragged him to a tree and bound him fast with rawhide thongs. "Burn him!" they shouted. "Burn him!" Other warriors piled dry branches by the tree. One brought a flaming torch.

All at once Tecumseh felt sick. He glanced at his brother. Chiksika looked troubled, but he did nothing to stop the warriors. The wood caught fire, and the Long Knife began to scream with pain.

"He is our enemy," Tecumseh told himself. "He *should* suffer." Somehow, though, Tecumseh could not believe this. The warriors seemed like wild beasts now, not friends he was fond of. They laughed, mocking the tormented man. Tecumseh could watch no longer.

As he turned away he felt Chiksika touch him. "I too am ashamed of this," Chiksika whispered.

"It is so cowardly," cried Tecumseh angrily.

Something inside told him that such cruelty was a sign of weakness, not strength. "Surely it is right for us to fight for our homeland," he thought, "but this cannot be the way."

"I am only a young warrior now," he told his brother. "But some day I will be a chief. Then I will put a stop to things like this. I swear it!"

4

A Warrior's End

During the next four years Tecumseh grew tall and strong. He went on many raids with Chiksika. More and more, other Shawnees came to admire them both. "They are two of our best warriors," the people said.

The younger brother, Lowalusika, was growing up too. He still was lazy, but his quick wit often amazed his elders.

"That one will be a great medicine man some day," they said. Such talk made Tecumseh proud.

Then came tragedy.

Chiksika and Tecumseh went on a hunting trip south of the Ohio River. The land there, called Kentucky, was an ancient Indian hunting ground. The brothers roamed far to the south and west. Never before had Tecumseh realized what a vast land he lived in. Everywhere, however, he saw the cabins of white settlers.

"Is there no end to them?" Tecumseh wondered. "They are like swarms of grasshoppers covering the land."

The Cherokee Indians who lived in that southern country were fighting the settlers. "We should go to help them,"

declared Chiksika. "These Cherokees are our friends."

Tecumseh nodded. "Yes, the Long Knives always help each other in battle and so must we."

The brothers joined a Cherokee war party in an attack on one of the settlers' forts. The fort was small and its log fence, or stockade, was not very strong. It stood in a field at the edge of a forest. Firing from the shelter of the trees, the Indians shot down many white men. At last the Cherokee chief commanded:

"Now! We will charge and climb over the wall."

As they broke into the open, a rifle cracked from the fort. Tecumseh heard a choked cry at his side. Turning, he saw Chiksika fall. He knelt at his brother's side, but it was too late—Chiksika was dead. Fury blazed up in the young warrior.

"Come on!" he shouted to the others as he sprang to his feet. "Don't stop! Attack! Attack!"

But the Cherokees held back. "You are cowards!" Tecumseh raged. "Chiksika has met a warrior's end. Are you afraid to die too?"

It was no use. The other warriors had lost heart. Sadly, then, Tecumseh lifted his brother's body in his arms and carried it into the forest. A deep, bitter grief filled him.

"I will never forget you, Chiksika," he whispered. "And I will never stop hating the white men. Never!"

5

Bad Times

Soon after Tecumseh returned to his home, scouts brought bad news. A great army of white soldiers was marching into Ohio country.

The word ran like wildfire through all the Shawnee towns. Warriors came riding from other tribes nearby—the Delawares, the Wyandots, the Miamis. "Meet with our chiefs in a council," they said. "The Long Knives threaten us too. We will help you to beat them once and for all."

Tecumseh felt a fierce joy. "Now I will avenge Pucksinwah and my brother Chiksika," he thought. He could hardly wait, as he sat in the big Shawnee council hut and listened to the chiefs make their plans.

Blue Jacket, chief of one of the Shawnee clans and a great war leader, stood up. "We will need a wise, brave warrior to lead our scouts," he said. "I choose Tecumseh."

"Hou!" cried the other chiefs. "We know Tecumseh. He is a good choice."

Quietly, yet proudly, Tecumseh rose to his feet. "I will do my best," he said simply.

Thus, in the year 1791, the war began. At first it went well for the Indians. Tecumseh's scouts followed every move the white army made. Then, one cold winter dawn, the Indian warriors attacked. Caught by surprise, the white soldiers fought badly. Many were killed or captured. Others ran for their lives.

Now Tecumseh remembered his vow. "We have fought bravely," he said. "Let us not spoil our victory by needless cruelty."

Many Indians would not listen. White prisoners were tortured and killed. "We have won!" the Indians cried. "That is all that matters."

They were wrong. Soon more white soldiers came. The war went on for four long, bloody years. Tecumseh, Blue

Jacket, and the other warriors fought on, but now they were outnumbered. They could no longer stop the white soldiers who marched wherever they pleased. Indian towns were burned, and their corn fields were destroyed. Families had to flee as best they could.

About a hundred Shawnee families, Tecumseh and Lowalusika among them, hid deep in the forest. They spent a hard winter there with barely enough to eat. In the spring a messenger came.

"The Long Knives offer us peace," he said. "We must go to their Fort Greenville to sign the treaty. Will you go with us, Tecumseh?"

"No!" Tecumseh answered. "No treaty will save our land from the white men. Their promises are worthless."

Discouraged though they were, his people cheered. "Tecumseh, you are our leader," they cried.

So it was that Tecumseh became the chief of his clan.

The messenger went away. Several months later Chief Blue Jacket rode into the village.

"The new treaty has been signed," he said. "This land belongs to the white men now. However, they will let us keep the land farther west, called Indiana Territory. They will build forts there and send a white governor. But the land shall be ours forever."

"Do you believe this?" Tecumseh asked angrily.

Now Blue Jacket shrugged his broad shoulders. "If we fight on, Tecumseh, we will lose everything. But this way, maybe most of the Long Knives will be satisfied."

Tecumseh thought of his father, and Chiksika, and other brave men who had died in battle. He bowed his head. "There has been too much sorrow," he thought.

"Very well," he said. "I will take my people westward. But remember—I have signed no treaty. We will see whether or not the white men keep their promise."

6

A Dream is Born

The Shawnees and their friends, the Delawares, were holding a council. The council pipe was lighted. Each warrior took a puff. A tall young chief stood up in the firelight.

It was Tecumseh.

Peace had lasted for three years. Tecumseh was thirty years old now. He had married a Shawnee woman named Mamate, but she had died, leaving him a baby son. The young chief was known among his people as a wise leader, as well as a strong, brave warrior.

Everyone listened carefully as he spoke: "Brothers, in our hearts we all know the treaty that was signed at Greenville was wrong. Our lands were given to us by the Great Spirit. No white man has the right to take them."

"Hou!" murmured the Indians. "It is so!"

"White settlers pour like a flood into our old homeland," Tecumseh went on. "Soon they will claim this land also. Do any of you doubt it?"

No one answered. Tecumseh picked up a twig from the ground and broke it in two. Then he gathered several twigs into a bundle and handed it to a

Delaware warrior. "Break that," he commanded.

The warrior tried, but the bundle was too strong.

"You see?" said Tecumseh. "One tribe alone is like one twig. But many tribes together cannot be broken."

Some of the young men nodded. "His words make sense," they told one another.

"A few tribes did band together to fight the Long Knives a few years ago," Tecumseh said. "And it is true that they were beaten." He paused. His voice grew deep and solemn. "But think how it would be if *every* tribe in this land joined one great Indian nation. There would be countless thousands of us. We could drive the

Long Knives off and win our old lands back. Nothing could stop us."

"Tecumseh, this is a dream," an old chief objected.

"Yes, a great dream," said Tecumseh proudly. "And we can make it come true." He lifted his arms. "It will take courage and patience, but we can be a proud, free people again. Who will follow me?"

"We will!" shouted several warriors. "Yes! Yes!" cried others.

Still, others were doubtful. But Tecumseh had made them think. In a few days, runners carried his words to more distant Indian towns. Everywhere, the Indians had been downhearted and discouraged. Now, because of Tecumseh, they felt new hope.

7

Tecumseh and the Prophet

Tecumseh's whole life was now devoted to his plan for a great Indian nation. He journeyed through the Indiana Territory and held councils with the Wyandots and Miamis. Farther west, he talked with the Sacs, Foxes, Potawatomies and the warlike Sioux.

"We will join you," their chiefs said. "Let us fight the Long Knives now!"

"No, we must bide our time," Tecumseh warned them. "Before we fight again, we must be strong enough to sweep every white man from this land."

The chiefs agreed to wait. Meanwhile a strange thing happened.

Lowalusika, Tecumseh's brother, had become a Shawnee medicine man. He had grown up into a small, rather ugly man, and few of the people paid much attention to him. Then a change came over Lowalusika.

First he adopted a new name, Tenskatawah, meaning One-with-Open-Mouth. The Great Spirit told him to do this, he said. From now on, he claimed, he would speak with the Great Spirit's voice. Perhaps he truly believed

44

this, for Tenskatawah began to preach to the Indians more strongly than he had preached before.

"Never be friendly with white men," he told them. "You must live clean lives. Be strong! Help one another! Above all, have faith in yourselves and in our great new leader, Tecumseh. The Great Spirit commands this through me—his prophet."

The Shawnees listened. Soon people from other tribes came to listen too. Tecumseh was very pleased. "Working together, brother, we cannot fail," he told Tenskatawah. "We must not—and we will not!"

Many Indians left their own tribes and came to join Tecumseh and the new prophet. So many came that after a while the two brothers moved to a new town on the banks of the Tippecanoe River in western Indiana. White men called the place Prophet's Town. These men wondered somewhat nervously what went on there. Yet several years passed, and the peace was not broken.

By 1809, as Tecumseh had foreseen, the whites were greedy for more land. The governor of Indiana Territory, William Henry Harrison, held council with a few chiefs from the Miami, Delaware, and Potawatomie tribes. He offered them whiskey, rolls of red cloth, food, and other presents. In return he asked them to sign a new treaty, giving up part of Indiana.

These chiefs were weak, foolish men.

They wanted these presents, so they signed the treaty.

Tecumseh's people were very angry. "Another white man's trick!" they cried. Others who had not believed Tecumseh before hurried to Prophet's Town. "You were right Tecumseh," they said. "We will join you now."

One day a white man appeared at Prophet's Town with a letter from Governor Harrison. The governor did not want the Indians to band together as they were doing. "If you try to make war again," the letter warned, "you will get nothing but misery and failure."

The white man read this aloud to all the Indians.

"Tell your governor that I will go

and talk this over with him," said Tecumseh.

More than 300 warriors went to Vincennes with their chief. White soldiers were lined up to meet them. Governor Harrison stood there—a sturdy, broad-shouldered man in a uniform trimmed with shiny gold braid. He had piercing dark eyes under heavy brows.

Tecumseh looked tall and stately in a fine buckskin shirt and leggings. He wore a red blanket around his shoulders and two eagle feathers in his hair. He and Harrison shook hands. The meeting began in a grove of trees outside the town.

"We come in peace, but we cannot be friends if you keep taking our land," Tecumseh declared.

"My government bought the land," said Harrison. "It is ours now."

"The land belongs to all the tribes," Tecumseh argued. "A few chiefs had no right to sell it."

They talked on, but neither man would yield. At last Harrison said coldly, "This meeting is over. I will tell the President of the United States what you have said, Tecumseh. He will decide about the land. I warn you, though—we mean to keep it."

The two men stared at each other. Each knew that he was facing a strong, bold enemy.

8

A Brother's Folly

Tecumseh hurried back to Prophet's Town. There he gathered twenty of his best warriors. "Quickly! We must make ready for a long journey," he commanded. Then he turned toward Tenskatawah.

"We have no time to lose," he said. "Governor Harrison has made it plain that we will have to fight to save this Indiana land. Most of the northern tribes will fight with us. Now I must get the southern tribes to join us too."

The Prophet's eyes gleamed. "Death to the Long Knives!" he cried.

"Patience, brother," said Tecumseh. "There must be no trouble until we are ready. I think Harrison may attack you while I am gone. If he does, take our people and run away. Promise me, Tenskatawah. I am counting on you."

"I promise," he answered gravely.

Tecumseh and his band rode far south into the land that is now Florida. All along the way the tribes knew of his great fame. They greeted him and his warriors joyfully. He held solemn councils with the Cherokees, the Creeks, the Choctaws, Chickasaws, and Seminoles.

"Everywhere I see white settlers," he told them. "They chop down your forests. They kill the wild animals you need for food. Soon they will take your land away altogether, and you will have nowhere to go."

"It is true," said the Indians sadly.

"We must stop them before it is too late," Tecumseh said. "Will you join your northern brothers?" Carefully he explained his plan for a mighty Indian nation.

"We will join," they agreed.

Tecumseh gave a packet of red sticks to every chief. "Each time the moon is full, burn one stick," he said. "When the last stick is burned, the Great Spirit will give you a sign. Then gather your warriors and march north to meet me."

"To fight?" asked some of the chiefs.

"When they see our great strength, the Long Knives may be afraid to fight," said Tecumseh. "Then we can have a fair and lasting peace. But if we must fight—we will!"

Only one chief hung back. This was Big Warrior, of the Creeks. To him, Tecumseh said scornfully, "When I return home I will stamp my foot. The earth will shake. Your village will fall down. Rivers will flow backward and the sun will hide his face. That will be the sign I spoke of."

Big Warrior became very frightened. "Tecumseh, don't be angry," he begged. "I will join you."

Finally Tecumseh rode homeward, well pleased with his work. As his men crossed the Ohio River, they saw a warrior from Prophet's Town waiting on the north bank.

"Bad news!" the warrior cried. "All is lost!" Quickly he told his story.

"A short time ago, Harrison marched toward our town with many soldiers. Your brother, The Prophet, disobeyed your orders. He urged us to fight. He told us he had magic powers. No white man's bullet could hurt us, he said—"

Tecumseh scowled. "Go on; and then—?"

"We were fools, Tecumseh. We really believed him. We attacked the soldiers, but The Prophet had lied. Their bullets killed many of us. The Prophet himself ran away. We all ran. Then Harrison's men burned Prophet's Town. . . ."

A hot, blind rage filled Tecumseh, but he controlled himself, with an effort.

"We have been betrayed," Tecumseh's warriors shouted furiously. "The false Prophet must die!"

"No, let him live with his shame," Tecumseh said. "That will be a worse punishment. Forget him. We must try to undo this harm he has done." But Tecumseh's heart was heavy. Would his followers stand by him now, or would they be afraid?

He did not know.

9

When the Earth Shook

From a new camp far in the woods, Tecumseh sent trusted messengers to the other tribes. Soon he knew the worst. Most of those tribes had lost their faith just as he had feared. They would follow him no longer.

Then a British officer in a red coat made his way to Tecumseh's camp. He came from Canada, the land north of the Great Lakes.

"My country, England, plans to make war on the Americans," he told him. "America once belonged to us. Then the Long Knives fought us and got their freedom."

"I know," Tecumseh nodded.

"Now we are going to win back this land," said the Englishman. "If you help us we will give all your old homeland back to you. Our king promises this."

Tecumseh talked with his few loyal warriors. "I don't trust *any* white man," he declared. "Still, these redcoats need our help. Therefore, they may keep their promise. I think we must take the chance. What do you say?"

"We say yes!" the warriors cried.

Later, that autumn of 1811, an

earthquake shook the land. Trees and houses tumbled down. The Ohio River flowed backward. Clouds of dust boiled up and hid the sun. It was the sign Tecumseh had described to Big Warrior, but it came too late.

The southern tribes had heard of Governor Harrison's victory over The Prophet. They were afraid to join Tecumseh now. Even the tribes nearby decided to wait.

The following June, England and the United States went to war. At once, Tecumseh led 70 warriors to Fort Malden, in Canada. "We have come to fight," he told General Isaac Brock, the British leader.

General Brock was a kindly and honorable man who liked the Indians.

He was a forceful, courageous leader, but he had only a few soldiers. Across the river which formed the boundary between the United States and Canada stood the town of Detroit. Many American soldiers were on duty there.

"They are too strong for us to attack," said Brock.

"No! Strike now!" Tecumseh urged. "We can capture Detroit." He took out his knife. On a piece of birchbark he scratched a map showing the best way to attack. The general was impressed.

"Very well," he said.

With his warriors and a few redcoats, Tecumseh crossed the river. The Indians hid in the woods around Detroit, cutting off all approaches by land. Now the town could not get help or supplies.

Brock then crossed the river with his men and prepared to attack. Tecumseh joined him.

Then Tecumseh ordered his Indians out of the woods. Whooping wildly, they circled round and round the town. The American general was terrified. He thought Tecumseh had many more men than he did. "We will all be scalped!" he told a frightened aide. So the general surrendered Detroit without a fight.

"No prisoner will be harmed," Tecumseh promised the Americans. "We show our manhood in battle, not by killing helpless people."

General Brock was so pleased with Tecumseh that he gave him a sword and a fine red coat. He took the silken sash from his own waist and tied it around Tecumseh's.

"Now you are a British general," he said.

Tecumseh smiled. He took the sash and gave it to another chief named Roundhead. "This honor belongs to all of us," he said. "Brother warriors, we have made a good beginning."

10

The Siege of Fort Meigs

Riding a big black horse, Tecumseh led more than 700 warriors out of Detroit. News of the great victory had brought Indian warriors hurrying to his side, eager to fight.

"We will never doubt you again, Tecumseh," they said.

British soldiers marched beside the Indians. The sun gleamed on warpaint and red coats. Muskets and tomahawks

glittered. Big iron cannon rolled along, pulled by straining oxen. The army was on its way to attack the Americans' Fort Meigs in northern Ohio.

Another British general, Henry Proctor, had taken General Brock's place. He was fat and haughty, and Tecumseh didn't like him. Still, the army was so strong that victory seemed certain. Tecumseh's heart beat fast with pride and hope.

Fort Meigs was a strong place, built of stones and thick logs. William Henry Harrison, Tecumseh's old enemy, was in command there. Cannon muzzles stuck out of the walls on every side.

"My cannons are bigger," General Proctor boasted. "We will knock this fort to pieces."

The British gunners fired. Again and again the cannons thundered. Through clouds of smoke, Tecumseh and his warriors attacked, but the Americans had held their fire. Now bullets and cannon balls flew from the walls. The Indians were driven back.

For two weeks the fighting went on.

Then more American soldiers marched up from the south. They fell on the British and Indians by surprise. But suddenly Tecumseh saw his chance. "Pretend to run away!" he cried.

The Indians ran, with the yelling soldiers in pursuit. The land was covered with dense woods and thickets. Soon the Americans were strung out in disorder. "Now!" Tecumseh shouted. "Turn and fight!"

The warriors, who had stayed together as they fled, turned and pounced on their enemies like wildcats. Rifle balls and tomahawks cut the Americans down. Some ran pell-mell back to Fort Meigs, but many threw down their guns and surrendered.

As they led their prisoners back to camp, the warriors were still filled with the madness of battle. Some of them began to kill the Americans. Tecumseh galloped up from the battlefield just in time. Leaping from his horse, he seized two warriors and flung them to the ground. He whipped out his warclub.

"Who dares to defy Tecumseh?" he roared.

The warriors shrank away in fear. Immediately the chief's terrible anger left him. "Have you forgotten my teachings so easily?" he cried. "Oh, my poor brothers—what will become of you?"

General Proctor had watched all this and he had done nothing. "Why didn't *you* protect these prisoners?" Tecumseh asked.

"Sir," replied General Proctor stiffly, "your Indians cannot be commanded." Actually, he had been afraid.

"Begone!" Tecumseh thundered. "You are unfit to command. Go and put on petticoats!" He turned away in despair. Proctor was a bad, weak man, he knew now.

For the first time, Tecumseh felt doubt. How could the British win a war with such a leader?

11

The Last Battle

General Proctor ordered his army to retreat.

"Do you expect to win by running away?" Tecumseh asked in disgust.

But the general would not listen. He marched the army all the way back to Detroit. Scouts brought word that William Henry Harrison was following with a strong American force. Still Proctor would not fight. He gave up

Detroit and led his men across the river to Fort Malden.

"I was wrong to trust the British," Tecumseh told his warriors bitterly. "They lie to us, like all white men. If you want to leave me now I won't blame you."

"No, Tecumseh, we still believe in you," the warriors said.

More bad news came. British and American warships fought a battle on Lake Erie. The Americans won. At that, General Proctor left Fort Malden and retreated again. But now Harrison's army was close behind.

Tecumseh went to Proctor's tent. He stood there tall and stern in his red coat. "You are like a dog that puts its tail between its legs and runs away," he said. "Go, then! My people and I will fight alone."

Stung by Tecumseh's scorn, General Proctor ordered his army to stop retreating. They were camped on high ground several miles north of Lake Erie. On one side ran a river called the Thames. On the other was a swamp. It was a good place to make a stand. But Tecumseh had lost hope now. He called his warriors together.

"Brothers, tomorrow we go into battle," he told them. "I will fall in that battle."

He unbuckled his British sword and handed it to a warrior. "Give this to my son when he grows to manhood," he said. He took off his red coat and put on a buckskin shirt. Watching, the

Indians felt their blood run cold. Somehow, they knew Tecumseh spoke the truth. But even now not one of them would leave him.

The next morning, the British and Indians lined up for battle. Across the field they saw their enemies coming. With a crash of rifles, the Americans charged. The British line broke, and General Proctor wheeled his horse and galloped off. British soldiers began to surrender.

Now a great mass of Americans on horseback came dashing toward the Indians' line. "Hold your fire till they draw near," Tecumseh shouted.

The rifles spat flame. Many of the Americans tumbled from their saddles, but the rest came on. The fighting raged back and forth. Tecumseh ran at a tall American officer, lifting his war club for a mighty blow. The American raised a pistol and fired.

There was a flash, a roar. Tecumseh fell.

"Tecumseh is dead!" At that dread cry, the Indians turned and melted into the surrounding forest. Suddenly the battle was over.

Late that night, says an old Indian legend, some Shawnee warriors stole back to the battlefield. Silently and sadly they bore Tecumseh's body to a spreading tree beside the Thames River. There, in a secret grave, they buried their great chief.

Tecumseh's dream of a proud, free Indian nation had ended forever.

Years of peace followed. The Indians lived as best they could in the white men's America which grew and prospered. As time passed, even the white men came to admire Tecumseh for his bravery and his high ideals. In a strange sort of way, their own nation was much like the one he had tried to build. Americans too believe in courage, honor and freedom.

Today we remember Tecumseh as a noble leader who gave his life for his people.